The Meaning of My Story 3

By: Marshay Herder

Brand: MarshayH-WithPassion2

Company: MarshayModels Entertainment

Table of Contents:

Module 1: It's not as it Appears

In life, we often judge without knowing, we look and we assume that we know what a situation really is and we are often wrong. Those we assume have it all together, are often suffering behind closed doors. We put ourselves in others shoes by saying what we would do without ever being in their position. We hear stereotypes and make them our truths without ever really getting to know you. I am sorry for every life I spoke on without knowing where you come from and who you really are but I'm human and my perception of who you are tainted my view of you. I remember being judged by girls at school who saw me and assumed I was a "bitch" then when they got to know me, they discovered I was sweet and easy to get along with. They aren't the only ones who judged, I probably judged them, too but I thank God for giving us the opportunity to find out who we really were. I apologize for the times I didn't give you a chance to show me who you are and I want to explore the pages of your book as you read mine.

The Hood Life:

Everybody has an opinion when it comes to little black kids raised in the hood

Everybody assumes their ghetto, rude, disruptive, loud and inhumane

Everyone chooses to assume they ain't gone be nothing, they can't succeed

Everybody has their minds made up and are stubborn to the idea of a good child, living the hood life

No one knows that every child they look at with disgust are far better off than us

The children they choose not to help, not show the right path can be the same children to make a drastic change in our world

Everybody loves to stick out mistakes of little black kids

Everyone figures these children chose the lives they are living

Everyone wants to blame them for this world's depression

Everybody loves to take the factor off race and pretend it's a coincidence of whom they blame

No one decides to stand up and help

The children ridiculed and never given a chance end up feeling that that's all they could do

I choose that the hood life is not what they were giving

The Hood Life is just the life they are living

A 'Nigga' Can't Do Nothing

At 1st I thought I was smart

Thinking I could actually make a difference in the world

But what a fool I am

Mama, Daddy, sis and bro, teachers, neighbors and friends

All say I'm foolish

They ask me who I see on t.v.

I say white folks

They ask me who I hear on the radio

I say white folks

They ask me what color is every money maker (legally)?

I say white folks

And they all say exactly

Then they chant A 'Nigga' can't do nothing

This repeated in my head several times

What little brain I do have

Thinking I would live in Hollywood and not the hood

I must've been out of my mind

(Crazy)

Sometimes I get a little delusional

Believing I'm something, I'm not

Thinking I'm somewhere, I can't go

Wanting to feel a way, I can't feel

Trusting someone who shouldn't be trusted

Loving something that couldn't receive Love

So, they make me think

And I figured just because that's the way things are

Doesn't mean they can't change

I listen to what they say and I use it to push me towards my goals in every way

Afraid

Sometimes I believe I am the one who puts fear in my head most

I am Afraid

I honestly can admit that I feel my head with false evidence appearing real

Many are skeptical of the future

Some are still stuck in the past

Afraid to live life each day

Struggling to pray

Fear can be the most difficult tribulation

And can cause trials throughout the nation

Afraid to step out on the limb afraid to believe in him

Sometimes people search so hard and climb so high

When what their looking for is finding themselves out first

Being fearful, it happens all the time

Don't allow it to cause you to run out of time

Showing fearlessness takes time because of your dark past

Or what's expected to be your future

Worry about nothing

Care about everything

Beat, Beat

Woman you ain't gotta' get beat

You ain't gotta' get beat, beat

Why you are sitting there when you can't do what you want

He ain't got nothing-nothing you need

You ain't gotta' get Beat, Beat

You are beautiful, you are smart

We are going show that man how to get your heart

So, take it back two steps, move it over to the right

Do it so good, he be looking all night

Shake it from the top

Then you bend over and drop

Pop, pop, pop, pop, pop

Now we are seeing who on beat

We rocking that beat, beat

Tell that man he betta keep his hand to himself

Cause he ain't going to hit u again

Cause we always on that Beat, Beat

You betta defeat, feat

Full Grown Woman

As soon as I was asked my age

Ten years because my mentality was past my physical years

A lot of pain, I've cried some physical tears

Age is counted by the days we live

Mine is counted by my mindset

When I see women of a certain age, filled with rage

The anger they need to control

The physical fight need to be put on hold

As they fight, I see them fighting for their mother's love

As they argue, I see them wanting a hug from their father

His presence couldn't be any farther

I feel for them one second then I stop

Being an adult means having the ability to grow and learn from a situation and not become a victim

To you I say Pray, Pray, Pray

and work on your emotions everyday

Fully Loved

My hair, My Make-up, My Nails, My skin

It's not what makes me, me

Is that all you can see

Treating me like you don't care

I'm here

Not hair

Can't you see true beauty?

Within me, do you know me?

Do you even care?

Tell me my inspiration...

Tell me my aspiration

Tell me my dream

You can't cause

It's all about

My hair, my make-up, My Nails, My skin

Fully Loved

Gone (off drugs)

Girl I'm so weak

I can't even speak

My words come out as a slur

My eyes are never busy

Having no place to see

I'm feeling crazy (it's insane)

Never thought it would get me this way

My family can't even recognize who I am

I'm getting so upset with him

Done it so many times, I can't even stop

I'm addicted

Smoking all around the clock

The relaxation level it has gave me has only made me nervous knowing
that it would let me

When they ask me what's wrong?

I pretend that I'm strong

Having no integrity, lacking strength and longevity

Gone into a distant place, I can't even see my face

I'm in an outer world called Space

Had Me but Now I'm Gone

Had a woman that would cook for ya

Had a woman who would talk to ya

Did everything to provide for ya

Treat me like I am worthless

As soon as I move on

Act like your torn

Beg me back

But when I ask you couldn't rub my back (fast to be on beat with line before)

Had Me but Now I'm Gone

You said you wanted a ride or die

You took a ride and let my heart die (fast like line before)

When I left you, you wanted to cry

I waved to you, Good Bye

Had Me but Now I'm Gone

I was your Honey Bun

And you were my Gummy Bear

How did we let our Love go there?

When you were with other females

In several different hotels

Come home acting innocent

Paying several different rents

In high school told me I was the cutest girl

In college, told me I rock ya world

I was your favorite girl

Had Me but Now I'm Gone

Hated On

See there are always people around you who try to put ya down

God will be there to pick you off the ground

Sometimes-failure hits you so often

It seems like success won't come your way

Knock your haters out the way

Tell em they ain't got nothing to say

You could have what I got

It only takes faith, passion and determination

So tell them could hate On

Me, I ain't worried

Can't you see

You look at my clothes and say all I do is waste my money shopping

You look at my hair and say I think I'm rocking

Let me tell what you say ain't stop

Don't Hate on

Cause I got it going on

Move on

Hate On

Module 2: Telling My Whole Life

I wrote my experiences from a young age and I am still writing. Some people have told me that I put my family business out there and some people have thanked me for my courage. I didn't begin writing with people who were healed in mind, I wrote from a place of pain and translated my stories to end with peace. I was prophesying over my dead situations and speaking life into things that seem to have lost its heartbeat. I was resuscitating myself from the grave, I didn't know I was buried in. I was living in a place of fear and not love, wanting help grow and change lives but not being transparent enough to do so. Now, that I speak they want me to be quiet but those are the same people who asked, "Why was I so quiet?" and I apologize to those who cannot handle my honest answers. I thank those who are growing with me.

<u>I Can See</u>

I believe that you can't believe everything that they tell you

How do you know if they'll just fail you?

Painful to hear but truthful my dear

U can't trust everybody cause' you don't know the true intentions of people

I can't be blind, you can't be either

You received your pain in places you'd least expect

Know it'll happen and you'll have regrets

I'd like to teach you

Give it over to God and be guided with your heart

I've Been (I am)

I've been abused

I've been used

I've been mistreated, talked about and lied, too

Oh, but who I am is defined by my strength

The pain of my mother was transcended through me

All of her sorrow caused my pain

I've listened to what u said

I've listened to what u wanted me to do

But Daddy, I'm sorry my imperfections hurt u

Only tried my best

Worked my hardest

My emotions ran high, expecting a high

Only to wake up to disappointment and life in disarray

What could I say

I am

Not

Who

I've

Been

I AM ME

Jail or Life?

I'm standing up front of my 'Life after Homicide' class, I begin by introducing myself. I tell them my history, work, and our goals with the business.

"Okay" Hello Ladies and Gentlemen, we're all here tonight because homicide has occurred to someone we all know and love, we're here to strengthen you and encourage that there is Life After Homicide.

I'm Christa Waltz. I'm a leader of several organizations, motivator speaker and author. Tonight, I'll start by saying my saying my story; I have no one in my family who is incarcerated. Wow, that's good they chant. Some say your lien. Then I say it's not as good as you think.

No one I know is incarcerated because their all dead.

They all gasp in shock. Sympathy begins to flow. Sobs continue. I began to speak "Don't cry for those who are going out, cry for those who are coming in". Raise your hand if you know someone who's incarcerated. All hands rose.

"You are blessed" I state. You are blessed because they are still here, there's still a chance, still an opportunity. So don't look at the situation with defeat, feel you have the ability to beat.

I had 3 brothers who had no second chance, shot and killed all on the same day. Now people say, wrong place, wrong time. It was right, god knew when, how, and where it would it occur.

Their time all at same time.

I had a niece, 19 years old, ran away from home, moved in her drug-dealing boyfriend home. Found dead three days later. They say she made him upset when he already angry because someone owed him money. Getting involved when you shouldn't.

My cousin found dead outside of 7- Eleven, she's 23, reason unknown.

I have no one incarcerated but everyone dead.

Pt. 2

"Now that I've talked about my instances and how we relate" I state. I want to hear yours.

Begin starting here....Introduce yourself....

Hello, I'm Barnaby Stic and my son killed by his choice of living life, he... I stop her, when you say choice of living, you mean. I mean he was gay-she blurted out. "O.k. similar to my 23-year-old cousin". The woman began crying, saying the man who killed my son was former son's friend and when out my son was gay, he stabbed him, he stated "he felt betrayed'. Investigators found out that he received 2 years of counseling because his father was gay and chose to throw him out to satisfy his gay partner. He had reported instances of endangering others.

O.k. Thank you. Next....

The next gentleman who states his granddaughter came to this country from Panama, four years to attend college. Three months ago, he came to visit her; there was an eviction notice on her door. He contacted everyone he knew and no one knew where she was. He went to the police station only to found out that she was hit by a tow truck driver. They say she was a prostitute. Running, chasing her pimp for her money when she was hit and killed.

Stories continued and tears flowed. At the end of the day, everyone expressed what they wanted. Everyone saw how they were not alone.

Life after homicide helped release built up emotions of pain and sorrow.

There is Life after Homicide.

Joyful Pain

I'm in the studio

Recording my song

When everybody stops and they turn and face me

I say everything's fine

They say we've never heard you sing so genuine

We've never heard it until the end

I say your mistaken joy for pain

Joyful pain

I can be on time, I can be on key

But the biggest thing is expressing me

Emotions shall be strong, it shall not take too long

Now don't think somethings wrong when you notice a change

Cause positive can come, negative can go

Joyful Pain

La La Land

'A bird doesn't sing because it has an answer, it sings because it has a song"

Such strange place

Never have I been here before, if so I've never lived in this town and it's been so long…

This residence must not be permanent

When I opened my eyes angels arise, questions in my head

I wondered what was ahead

Like a brand-new World

I entered not knowing what to expect

2 my surprise

I believed I BELONG HERE MOST

It was my peace, my sanity, my hope and

Love

That helped me rise above

Finally, the person I wanted to be

A place in my life where I was happy

Love Confliction

It will never be the same (same, same)

If you keep playing this game (game, game)

You take me as a fool (fool, fool)

You think that you rule (rule, rule)

You always acting so cruel (cruel, cruel)

You think our situations cool (cool, cool)

Let me take a breather

Let me step back

Let me tell you-how you lack

You aren't moving on, adding on'

Love Confliction, My addiction

I know the tribulations of my situations

Ain't making life no easier, only adding to the stress, making me feel less

Covering up my inner insecurity

Only to pretend you're my security

Whole time you were weak

Love Confliction, My addiction

Major Problem

Major problem wasn't me getting by a bus saving my sister's life

Losing my leg and kidney

Major Problem were the boils and the fierceness within me

I felt a bump or a lump and I cried

But At least I was still alive

Living healthy

To me I was dying

My soul was burning and the inside of me was crying

Ca ne fait rien

That I'm hurt still because forever this child will be hurting until

She exits earth and has her day of rebirth

But

She saved a life

All because of Love

Major Problem, wasn't major at all

MBS

My mind, Body and Soul can never be controlled

I am Me, don't you see

My Mind, Body and Soul shows my passion, let's go of my pess-i-mist

I am Me, can't you see

My Mind, Body and Soul is ready to help who I can, do all that I can

I Can

I am not weak

The weak I do seek

Wanna help em' all

Never you let you fall but your mind, Body and Soul is in control

What it is that's true, is deep inside of you?

No one can snatch it out, someone can reach out

Be what you can

Try and Do you

We love your mind, body and Soul

<u>*My Heart*</u>

I'm a let u know, there isn't no way I can let you go

My God, you'll always be in my heart

Will never be separate or apart

Cause you are a part of my heart

When I'm down and feeling low

You see me moving real slow

You always find a way to make me have a better day

Giggle or Laugh, not in need of no cash

I am so stubborn at times and other days I won't be quiet

Because of my fire

My burning desire

Makes me feel like I'm on a wire

Attached to a tire

What a heavy load…that's the only time I move slow

Other than that, I'm ready to go… ready to show

Can't wait till' they know

My Joy

(Not you Boy!!)

I only loved you for a day and you gave my love away

So many others would say

That I was - Crazy

Wanting to be near you

Wanting to call you my boo

I never quite expressed the way I felt

Being near you made me want to melt

Away from you I wept

The desire for a man's love

I needed help

I had my father as a child so that wasn't that

It was the kid who would call me fat

Boy you told me I was beautiful, I only believed you

You break my heart

Left me alone and depart

My joy is not from you boy

Module 3: Look at How It All Turned Out

I know with confidence that every dream I've had will once be my reality. People around me think that I am crazy for believing that a nine to five will not be my career, I think I am bold for taking a chance on myself, for my family. I am willing to risk being mocked, made fun of and talked about in order to push for what I really want. I believe God is going to make my dreams come true and the devil is mad now for things that have yet to happen in my life. Now how funny is that to think, I already have people who once laughed now standing in line asking how I did it. My message to you is "Take a Chance on You." No one will take a chance on you like you can, no one will invest what you can for you, believe in who God created you to be. You are the only version of you to exist, even if you have a twin, an identical twin with the same DNA, God has a divine purpose for your life!

<u>Near God</u>

O, I wanna move near Jesus

O, I wanna move with my lord

My god, let's get closer my god, let me know ya

O, I wanna face you Jesus

O, I wanna feel you my lord

Strengthen my soul

Broaden my heart

Care for me from the start

Strength behold you, lord I told you

Caring for me like I know is impossible

Beginning

On Fire

I luk at you and wonder why you so red

I luk again and say you're a hot head

Go ahead

Lose your mind

Waste your time

This time as the temperature rose

It rose above your toes

And touched ya knees

Like a plant to a seed

But Without the Weed

Each chance you had

You promised your dad

He'd be better than the last

That abuse was a part of ya past

But lies was all you told

He locked you down and got your child on hold

Watching as the fire rose

Crying-----Whining-------Because of all your lying

You were Dying

Relief

I've been holding on too long

It's like I'm singing a song

It's like a melody

It's like a tune

It's like the coming moon

Recording each beat

Humming each tone

Until I get into the zone

Feels like an hour

Feels like all day

Only been 20 minutes

When it's finished and completed

Back to normal things

No more room to sing

I've been holding –zone

No more time to wait

Almost time to wake

Gotta get up, be prepared, do my hair

I have been waiting so long, it's like I'm singing a song

Moving up, Moving faster

I gotta wait until I get unto the zone

<u>Hairdo'</u>

You know when a girl got a new hairdo

You know she carries' a new attitude

Her swagga's at its highest point

And she is flaunting is that joint

Got the face done up

Got the heels too high

Got a smile on your face

Got that power and grace

It's a new hairdo with her new attitude

Getting extra attention with facts to mention

It's compliments coming in her ear from every place she's near

Getting confident, gaining strength

Women-Can't -Stop-

When-That –Hair- Is- Did

You betta compliment that woman just like she deserve

It takes a real man to have that kind of nerve

Women could tell it from the start

They could read your heart

Hair…. Do….

You Cannot Stand

trying to be ahead of the game
cooking, providing and kissing someone's butt
thinking that it would cause them to feel like you are perfect
and it's all to feel a void
that you have for a lack in another place
but the same person's ass you kissed, smack's you in the face
giving no second thought about you
but the one who's there and hasn't gone anywhere is treated less than
and not stretched above and beyond for
but why they say?
simply because you claim them to be
important to you
when the God's honest truth is
they are a reflection of their father
the same father, you cannot stand

<u>Stupid One</u>

Don't forget how far we've come
Don't forget all the work we've done
Don't forget all the time we spent
Don't forget when I paid your rent
It's sad
That you no longer consider me a friend
After all the time
The ways
The games you played
I stayed
And you called me stupid
And I had the nerve to think you were the stupid one
Thinking I was smart
For keeping a job
That I basically work for you
Because every time I turn around
I'm giving my money to you
Too many times I've lied to my mother when she asked what was I doing with my
money
When I needed her to spend her money on me
I was too ashamed to say I helped you
Who I did not live with
I love, have kids with and that was all
Because what I thought what we had, I later found out was not much at all
I feel ashamed for thinking I was the one
I was one out of them
There was her and her and her, too
You did a good job of making me feel special at times
I will admit
But I was too stupid to see, it was not legit
You picked the kids up from school and met me later at work
I thought you spent your time with the kids
When I realized it was her kids, I could hear playing in the back
And you had the nerve to make me think I was not enough
That I didn't cook enough
And love on you enough
When you didn't deserve a drop of my love

Not a dime
Not a minute of my time
That I continued to waste on you
I am
Angry
For accepting less than I deserve
I am
Angry
For having the nerve to think you were giving me all you had
Which was not enough
It is not me who was not good enough for you
It was you who had me convinced that was all you could do
It didn't mean I had to accept It
but I did and I had my father around
My mother, too
So, there was no sad story to tell
I am just a girl, naive enough
To accept a piece of shit
And that is YOU
I am crazy, a fool
I am the stupid one

Bliss

I smiled at you when you grabbed my face

I laughed at you when you walked away

I wanted you around

You make my belly dance like its New Year's Eve

You make my heart jump like a frog on a leap pad

You are strong like my dad's knee before it went bad

You look like my uncle who all the women say are fine

You give me moments I want to bottle up in time

Capsules so that I can open and be reminded

Of what we once were

I am in love with you

This is what they call Bliss

Unity

I look at you like I look at water

You are my source of life

You are good for me

And I take you in

You are my refresher

My Best Friend

You make things come out of me

That I didn't know exist

You flow so effortlessly just like this

I need you everyday

And there is no way

That I would still breathe without you

You are mines

And I wouldn't want it any other way

Trust

You trust him before your girl

And the first chance he gets to snitch on you

He does

You choose time with him

And the first time you're in a bind

He can't help with a dime or time

But it is her that you call

And she answers

She gives without question

You lean on him but when you're not around

He treats her differently

You grind they say

You make a way

But trust me, if there was as much work being put in as they thought

You would not have to beg and that's law

Module 4: Rescue Me

Has your life been difficult? Have you struggled to get up, get out or start a new venture that you want? In life, we will often be buried in problems, debt, pain, sadness and grief. It is my belief that these moments always end, change or pass by. This process can be hard to experience but there is a god, that will rescue you every time. Prayer is pivotal in my life, I pray than release and I watch positive changes occur in my life. I needed saving more than once in my life and I am not ashamed to say, there were very few who were there to help me grow while some left me during my sink. You must stay close to those who honor you in the moments where you aren't honorable. They deserve the best of you and have prayed during your worst moments.

Trees

Trees they stand mighty and bold

Being strengthened through the cold

Standing tall nothing to hold

Providing the oxygen for us all

Giving us a breeze before the sun falls

Never being taken down, living still with a crown

Trees hold on to their roots

Letting many leaves fall

Broadcasting over a long range

Trees are powerful in so many ways

All of them couldn't be stated in this poem I made

Through trees we see more clearly

We see everything from on top

Trees have feelings, they have a heart

Nothing has to pass by or say 'hi'

Trees never bow goodbye

Trees are themselves

They have a personality

My tree is a tree that we all see

Bring You Down with Them

Many people get depressed, worried or stressed

The mood around them is naturally gloomy

They pretend to be o.k. but really feels pressured throughout the day

A Love is missing, that they're trying to find

Pretending that it's there the whole time

Wanting to explore something new

Confused and worried about their thoughts

Not caring about one's own happiness

Are you truly happy?

Can you truly find love?

They exude the sadness to all whom their around

Pretending to stand one's ground

Making the situation worse than it is

Trying to have others support on their weird, crazy thoughts

Having battles, having mental and physical faults

Bring you Down with Them

Trying to have you sad, trying to make you mad

No one can smile unless they are

These people truly are insecure

Needing to search within

Needing to find a friend

Someone as an extra caretaker

Someone like a nanny

There for their comforting needs

They keep on fallen'

In and Out of Love

Loving the temporary misery state

Moser Loves Company and Your Just the Company They need

__Ambition__

I got ambition

Living life on a mission

Never stepping down, but I keep stepping

I got a lot of work on my mind

Working all the time

Showing how I care

Practically living there

My business is my life

I put up with all its strife

Continuing to stay strong

Identifying when I'm wrong

Don't got no time to pout or cry

The road never stops, my mission never dyes

If ever frozen, stuck or confused

I need a laugh to keep me amused

Life goes on with

Ambition

<u>I Rule</u>

I Rule

There ain't going be no abuse

There ain't being no misuse

Cause I Rule

There ain't no talking no trash or I'll kick ya ass

If you got something to say, you betta come correctly

Too much of a woman

Too strong of a soul

I'm in control, ain't trying to be ya momma

Not looking for no drama

I'm just letting you know

Ima be in control

It's my life and I'm going to live

(instruments solo)

Cause I rule

African Americans

African Americans may seem like it's all bad

Like everyday life is sad but just know it's the name

Of your race and the color of your face but it

Does not determine your future goals

African Americans are beautiful and they just don't know

There smart and talented, too

One thing is in the way and it's you

Each person must stand up and believe for African Americans to achieve

We have dreams and they will come true

It all depends on the attitude of you

Decide if you want to be behind this race

For it is beautiful and can have great fate

Dream Imposter

Dream Imposter

Dreaming 2 be the next Kobe, Shaq or LeBron

Dreaming to be the next Monica, Brandy or Mya

Not able to dribble a ball, not able to sing a note

Having a dream that will become denote

Creating someone unreal, whose lifestyle will be reviewed and talked about every time they eat a meal

Soon changing unto somebody no one ever knew, doing things the people thought the person couldn't do

Lying to himself, family and the world

Letter shocking to himself to who he really was believing wealth and fame could change whoa person really is

Only to see the reality of how the situation really is

Love

Love is infinite, it doesn't end

Love to me is like a friend

Except with love it never ends

Love is powerful and can override any obstacle

Love who you want and make sure it stays

Every night and Everyday

Love is strong and its dynamite

Love is the best, but also can be a mess

Love is and will not end

And always will be

Forever a Friend

School

School is a place to focus

School is a place to you go

Learn and learn so you can walk

Out the door with a better education and way more determination

Know who you are

For you may be a genius or superstar

Flame

Flames around me

You watched me burn

My respect you will never earn

A man knows how to protect

You were nothing but a reject

When you saw that first fire start to build

You should've been there as my shield

For I had to yield when I was on fire

When that first fire came you were not my burning desire

F L A M E

Wasn't Quite

You loved what you saw
You loved what you heard
But didn't even know the truth about her
That's why you couldn't understand why she responded the way she did
Didn't know she had that much in her head
Looks can be deceiving at times
Never listened to the lyrics in her song
Only tried to get in her thong
You were wrong, that you can't do
I'll tell you it is true; I only give it up if I fall in love with you
That I cud never do
You thought my body was hot, thought you'd find my spot
But I won't allow it
Sorry!!
I wasn't quite what u thought
Wasn't Quite nothing but Dynamite

Module 5: Devastation

Disappointment leads to devastation. Devastation is a cause of severe shock, distress and/or grief. Devastation can cause physical sickness. We often experience turmoil that lasts sometimes minutes to years, they shape who we are in a way. We are no longer as open, loving, friendly and accepting as we once were. This is not always a major issue but can be a problem when are unable to disconnect ourselves from the pain we once experienced. It is not always going to turn out how we want, we must learn that setbacks happen but we do not have to stay stuck in devastation forever.

Trading

Cause if you wanna go

You are moving too slow

I don't wanna see u no more

Go out the door

Bye, bye

I don't wanna see u no more

U walked out of my door

Like God says when one door closes…another one opens

Never knew our relationship was doing so bad

It is getting to the point where it's sad

You left to go pursue your career goals

Left your family, including your kids

Do you understand what you did?

That was so Disrespectful

Trading places, Trading spaces

Repeat beg lines

Don't know what u left behind

Don't know what u thought was coming

God doesn't bless those with wrong intentions

Also, to mention

You missed out on m

Rule the Air

Heaven is only but so far

I thank you for what you've done this far

You created a star

If you stay on this path

God's strengthening power will last

He does not judge you by your past

Rule the Air

No judgment there

God says soar, you will score

He says "try", don't be afraid to fly

Never know what opportunity might come

Enjoy and have Fun

Rule the Air

<u>Hurry</u>

You don't have to worry

I ain't in no hurry

You just take your time

Life is short but long enough

To not hurry or worry

About things that don't matter

It'll be alright

Life doesn't wait on you

But you have time to do what you wanna do

<u>Sad Day</u>

I can make a gray day turn blue

I can make sad come out of you

I can make you feel so good

You'll be focused just like you should

I can make you realize your fate

Do you know it's not a mistake?

Sadness is what you make it

Live Life like it's the end

Know sadness is not your friend

Teach it that it can't beat you

You are the strongest, it's true

And all that sadness can't win against you

Have brighter day, smile in a better way

Learn that you are great

Sadness is not in the way

Believe in God in every way

You don't need no man

It ain't going to' change

You will still be so strong

So, don't get it confused

You don't need any man

To satisfy your life

To give ya' happiness

You are talented in so many ways

If you do it on your own

What's so wrong?

They act like it's so bad

But the true situation is sad

You live your life with a messed-up man

Who ain't doing nothing but trying to befriend

Men can get wasted

Be so waste less

So why waste your time

Women too, it' the same with you

A man could play games so well

Take you through hell

Never get it together, you are independent

Not dependent

You've Pleased

You've pleased the world

You've pleased me, who else can you please

I can't see

You gave me joy

OH

You've made me proud

Not only me but the crowd

I now stand and say

No more stress comes my way

I'm too blessed

I only pray

My God your victory has come to me

You've made my world

I have no reason to complain cause days you've pleased me

Are more than days I'm sad

You've pleased the world

You've pleased ME

Who else can you please?

<u>Soon</u>

Soon I'll be tired

Of waiting on you

To try to change

And be in my range

I've took up with your stuff and I've had enough

Life's been rough and tough

You've made it worse

I let you which I was stupid of doing

Soon

Soon I'll be tired of waiting on you

To try to be someone you're not

To doing things you'd never do

I've fallen out of love with you

I'm so sorry Boo

I no longer have that love for you

Soon

You'll see what you missed

You'll realize you want a kiss

But I'll just diss

You Baby

Sorry you lost out on a lady

Soon

Sooner than Later

I'll see ya' later

Baby: Fantasia B.

Been through so much

In your young years

Had so many people in your ears

Suggesting-Deciding-Choosing

Instead of listening to God

You listened to your heart

Left you in a lonely place

Didn't leave to you saw your baby face

You came back to Reality

To show your reality

Challenges face you

Devils always chasing you

Trying to ruin who you are

By dimming your star

He knew the areas you were weak

Your faults he did seek

In this sink, the water leak

Tears stream down your face

As you think back "why u have to live"

Because your child's a gift

Childish Memories-Desperate Days

Wake up-clean your Face

The devil tried to stop you

But he couldn't

So please keep moving on

I need u Baby

Sing that Song

A Testament

A testament of your strength

God tested you every day of your life

He already knew what you would do

When you would do it and why

A testament of your faith

Would you trust him in your time of need?

Would it be his phone number you called?

Or would you fall?

Only calling on God once you touched the ground and was down

Would you lift somebody else up

Or push em around?

__Bloodline__

Is it the bloodline or the love line?

To have a crush on a cousin

To not understand

Why you feel this way?

Come on Now

Get Real

It's me Shay

I know people front and hide

But I know your emotions on the inside

I'm not completely physic

But what I see is a feeling towards someone whom you'd give this feeling to anyone

Just to feel like someone's listening

In the end, you hear your pain a whistling

Will you continue to let your love go on missing?

And keep on kissing

Dig Out a Hole

He dug into my soul

The way he could speak so sweet and act so meek

It was all a treat

A treat I wanted to eat

Take a bite of delight and enjoy each piece

Took me to dinner

Talked to me about his goals

How he wanted me in his future

I was a part of his sole

We were almost there

I was in my gown

He was in his tux

But there was one thing that got UNtucked

The secret he held of how he carried Aids

Good I decided to be abstinent

For the disease I love its absence

No hole to dig out now

It would've been too deep in the ground

Due Season

A miracle is at your door

Will you get up and open it?

Or ignore the constant noise you hear?

Are you too lazy to realize?

Here lies…Your Miracle

It's your due Season

But you feel like your faith isn't due yet

Come on now, the time is not up to you

I don't care if you were resting

Would you rather your dream continues to nesting or turn out you receive less than

That's why you'd stand up and feel like you deserve more

For what?

Did you score?

Get off the Road

Get off the road

In this lane, you're driving too slow

The difficult pace makes you no longer a part of the race

Look at your face

Are you defeated?

If so, put your feet in their face and tell em' to eat it

It might be their dinner, they need it

Some people think that fast is cool

Some people think that leaning back, eating snacks

Go on and relax

But if you lack, it's o.k.

Getting stronger, better the next day

Get off the road of destruction

Join the rod of production

Hallways

It ain't going always be good

Sometimes it will be bad

Really bad

It may be rough

It may be tough

It may be long

It will be short

But it will be

Because life connects you to me

And this is the only way it should be

By Now

I bet you this paper has had enough

It's probably screaming "I can't take no more"

The same thing my mind screams every day

I don't understand how you are a grow woman who cries like a baby

But you claim to be a lady

Brag to every person that passes by

Like you've done so much but if only they knew how much it took just to get you
to do one thing

You are the worst example of what should be

That I've

Get This Off My Chest

I said I gotta get this off my chest

Sick of all the extra stress, I promise you it's really not worth me feeling this way

Especially when I was having a good day

I'm just sick of the fake, Everything is okay

Sick of the I guess this is the way

When honestly this road were on, is not doing anything for anybody

I can't take the it's okay, it will be alright

I use to hear that as a child some nights

Every time there was yelling and screaming, then I would see him swing

And there was always a sit down, it's going be ok, I promise I'm going change the way

Everything is going to be ok

Those words to me are fake

I don't see anything behind them but lies and mistakes

If you honestly feel some type of way, you should be able to express it, recognize

it as your truth and keep it moving but instead you'd rather put on a facade

Like your heart isn't hard

I'm getting this off my chest but I think it's something you need to get off yours

Module 6: NO

No means no, even in Spanish. This tells me there should be a level of respect between two people that you do not cross. If you want to engage sexually with a person and their response in no, do not engage anyway. Respect a person's response. If you ask to use a person's vehicle and their response is no, taking it anyway is stealing. If you ask someone to do something and their response is no, you need to respect their decision and choice. Don't force anything on anyone, that do not want.

Have you ever met someone so crazy?

But they call me crazy, maybe you haven't met this woman I know
She's crazier then all you folks, she can gently kind and wave her HI's
But oh, you won't get a goodbye
Without a storm that arrives
She seems so friendly and upbeat to some
Listen to those whispers that are louder than them
He may be the one and only who others can't believe
But oh' Marshay listens to the sounds of those who grieve
Who get down on their knee
Because I know there's some truths in what they say
And if there weren't, maybe they wouldn't be that way
The way that they are, it isn't for no reason
Make sure you pay attention to her winter season, not just the summer falls
Because before you know it, she'll spring back into action
And act all brand new, you'll be wondering if this is a new season, you knew
nothing about
No, that's just same ole her getting ready to scream and shout!!!!
This person's behavior may seem unusual to you but for me it is old news
It's just like her nightmares, they come out of her now why she's woke
And the funny thing is, she doesn't know what type of spirit of evokes
All but anything for FOLKS
Her life motto, let's see where it takes you
Cause I'm not getting ready to follow

He wants me but...

He wants me but he's not my type
Not what I like-- I say
Not what I need-- I could see it in the look in his eyes
But am I fallen for a Jekyll and hide
Am I following for what I'm attracted to
Because of my pride
Or will I finally listen to the voice inside
That says try
Have I not tried because I feel that either way, it isn't worth
Or it won't work
Am I wishing bad without even trying to enjoy the good
Am I just another girl who love u for the way u look
Do I not feel like I deserve better
Or so I see this as better because I'm not being abused, and I'm not being used so if
anything I'm doing good
But it is who girls don't look at twice
Dress nice and smells good, works a great job and drives a nice car
But his face is a little off
Body is a little off
Height is way off
From what you imagined so you walk pass him every day
Never speaks when he says "Hey"
All because he doesn't look like u like
And u keep telling yourself something ain't right
When really something isn't right with you
For thinking that a face and size is what makes the man
Not knowing if really he can protect your family
Care for the kids
Provide, even for a child that isn't his
Only time ever tells
You judge them by what you'll see
Forgetting to see them for who they really are

And you miss out on something great
All because looks is like sexy food on a dinner plate

<u>Childhood Friend</u>

He said he didn't like me anymore
To his childhood friend
Who was now my best friend
And could my heart break any more than it did in that moment
I prayed for his true feelings to be revealed
Thought that I would hear something else from somewhere else but I should've
known how funny God is
That he would send the person who I made fun of for liking my cousin
To tell me that I am not his type
My ears heard him but my heart denied that it was true
Just thinking to myself, how could the man I gave a key
To an inner part of me
Not be feeling ME
I just couldn't fathom to think that he came around me and everything I felt was
fake
Everything he said was like he said flaky
My mind couldn't imagine that he pretended to be
And I kept thinking to get what out of me??
I just couldn't see what it was
It's not like we ever made love
So I began to feel like I wasn't good enough
Maybe I wasn't skinny enough for him
Maybe my hair wasn't pretty enough for him
Maybe I just wasn't pretty enough for him
Then, I started thinking maybe I should've hugged him
And kissed him and loved him more
Maybe I kept opening up the wrong door
I was unlocking my heart when maybe he wanted my draws
And yeah, for my heart to open you gotta push, pull and tug
But when it opens up, it's nothing but love
And I know we're grown, 21, I am
And at this point his penis is sticking up and my panties are wet

So it's no longer boy and girl love like when we first met
I took up for him against everything negative anyone had to say
Put some respect on his name, I didn't play
I wonder if for me he would do the same
Got sick and tired of playing the guessing game
He likes me like he says
But what does he show
His inner true feelings, I had to accept that I may never know because then my prayers changed
I didn't want our love to change, I just wanted to hear it from his mouth and look in his eyes
And see, Is there ANY chance in hell he still wanted me??
My confidence started to say, Marshay, there's no way that you aren't good enough for him
Maybe, he isn't good enough for you
Then, I thought of the few reasons God could be keeping him away
But then I'd say
You like him and you aren't afraid to admit
And if he likes you, you'll know
If he doesn't, it'll show
Don't worry, Let Go
Your self-esteem had to go through this transition to grow
Transition to know
That everything is going to work out exactly like it should
And if he's a childhood friend, AT Least the memories are good

Guests

One after another

They come on my show

Telling their stories of partners, they need to let go

Passion they show

Choices they know

Are not right

They fight

But light

Please be at the end of the tunnel

We cannot continue to suffer

The fumble

The rumble

The trouble

The lies

The truth

They hide

Show

I'm watching it

The problems they have

Are all too familiar

I know

La Familia

I don't want to be a baby momma

I don't want the drama

I want a husband

My kid's father

To be the same person

Is that too much to ask?

The time waits

The lag

I beg

Of you God

Please

Can this be for me?

Capture

I am not keeping track of every single thing you do

Don't make that to be true

I don't write every tale, every fail, and every hell

I capture moments

In time

I write

I rhyme

I live

I love

I give

I trust

But I am a storyteller

Yes, this is true

You may end up in a book

So, watch what you do

<u>Remember Me</u>

I make you smile

I make you laugh

I make you work

I make it easy

I make you jump

I make you dance

I am the reason

Your life

Second Chance

Module 7: GRAND

I believe that I am grand. My thinking is grand. My life is grand. My faith is grand. My god is grand. My business ideas are grand. My abilities are grand. My talents are grand. My joy is grand. My writing is grand. My thoughts are grand. My talents are grand. My abilities are grand. My peace is grand. My sister is grand. My book is grand. My hearing and seeing is grand. My health is grand. My body is grand. My love is grand. I am built on the ideas of a grand god who decided to put two people together in a brief moment of time, to create me. My life is grand.

Good Girl

"My hair is wooly
And my back is strong
Strong enough to take
The pain, inflicted again and again"

I never thought
This time, this year
I would feel like I did last
Afraid everything, I enter never lasts
Afraid every time he enters, it's the last
I never thought
This time, this year
I would be releasing another book soon
But the last one still hasn't sold like I expected it, too
I am not stopping
This is my truth
Yet, I still don't see me giving up
On me
Because I believe
That this too shall past
And I won't write this same thing next year
With the hopes of something new
My business, my vision is growing
And I'm sowing my seed
Right now, I am a queen
With a crown
That does not fall off
It tilts, it tips, it dangles, its hung
But this is not the end
Of an everlasting journey
This is the engine
Being revved up and I'm about to go
To a place rarely traveled
Many do not know
But I
I am a queen
that is not afraid to say

I don't have the answers sway
I don't know the way
I am not stopping here
Their doubt I can't use as fear
I am a winner
And it is almost time for you to see
Me
everything you thought was done
Just begun
My journey, my path
This won't be my last
Strike on my back
But like a Nike stripe
I'll just do it
Like it's easy to be done
They don't know the battles I've won
I fight silent storms that no one can hear
I am so glad to be still hear
Out of every-thing I've experienced
I am full
And starving for more
I'm a queen goodness
The one you adore

All Eyez On Me

When they read a story on me
It's going be the truth they see
PAC passed the torch to me
Gave me the light and the message
His story, his strength --- I respect it
His love, his pain, his hurt
I felt it
I feel like I could feel it each time
Even though it happened before my time
I hear it in his rhymes
I hear it in the crime
He didn't get a record until he had a record
Still people can't see what they're really trying to hide
Philando Castile, dead life they can't deny
Mad as hell is not an expression
It's our truth, as black women with all these pent- up emotions
What are we to do?
They no longer carry whips and chains
But badges and claims
As they feared for their lives
But how are we supposed to feel inside
As a black man scared to survive
They been killing us for years
Separating our families
Young man walking down the street
Jay walking is what they claimed to me
As my life laid on pavement
Blood on his hands
That was the plan
Neighborhood watch
More like a crooked ass cop
I could see one
But one, two, three, too many
They say they fear us
But we don't have the guns in our hands
Uniform and the badge
To cover up the murders we commit

Too many lives I'm convinced
Tired of seeing us still living
Their purpose behind slavery was to make us all extent
Like dinosaurs, they wanted us to be a mystery
A myth, but the scars we still carry
On our backs, on our hands
Ankles and wrists in chains
Minds in bondage, not allowing us to grow
We can read now but they make further education cost more
So, we can still get no as an answer and not be able to walk through the door
So easily
We are sometimes looked at as if we don't try
But there's not another race on earth who must struggle as much as we do
Who must beg just to be
Accepted into this cruel world we call society
All Eyez On PAC
Black lives killed by a cop
Nothing new
When is it going to stop?
Can't keep begging for change
As we praying to gain
Changing the game
That we wish to do
Barack Obama, I take my hats off to you
Great job my brother
Tupac would agree
You are like the presidential version of me
I just want to see our children smile
I want to walk through the crowd
And not fear my chances of going home
Every time I'm on the road alone
Bullseye, they hit the mark every time
We're in caskets, all black at a funeral
It's all black cause we're all black
Are we all back to the same ole shit
Master, please
Raping our women while we're on our knees
We couldn't protect you then but we should now
Black men, she is the source of life
Respect her, she is your wife

Chances are that we still succeed
And they can't see how
You can push us
But we will not break
No restroom breaks
Our breath they take
We ate
Anyway
And yet we still exist
So, tell me how much more of this???

Award of Excellence

Women don't ever take the time to acknowledge so I will

I interned for Idol Mag

I interned for Mayor McDuffie

I interned for EZ Street

I interned for Baller Alert

I interned for Tressa Azrael

I attended a Microsoft certification course

I attended a business course

I attended an IT Audit class

I attended a blogging for business course

I attended a basics to photography class

I received my high school diploma

I received a medical assistant diploma

I work with Diva By Cindy

I work with R'Daugett Catering

I self-published two books

And this is my third

I am proud of the accomplishments I have

At 22, I've sat in rooms with women twice my age

I've had conversations with women with longer resumes

And I am just touching the surface

As Taraji would say

I am on a journey

And as young woman, I am leading the way

If no one is proud of what I've done, I will say

I am

I have a great relationship with God

I have a great relationship with my family

I have a few friends

I should be a trending topic

That never ends

And this isn't to be braggadocios

But this is to say

That the little girl from Temple Hills

Is making a way

For other young women to see

That I come from where you come from

And you, too can be

An Award of Excellence

All on your own

<u>Private</u>

Let's keep it between us

Please don't say anything to

I want to keep this between me and you

I don't need everyone in my business

What we discuss

This is for us

Can you handle that?

Sounds like me

Always keeping things between him and me

Never spreading lies

Never saying more than a person should know

I whisper

I hide

I keep my feelings inside

Until

Well I still won't say the whole truth

You can push

Tug

But I keep my promises

Especially to you

I just wonder

Have you done the same?

Or are you whispering my secrets?

Protecting yourself in shame

Is it just a game?

That I decided to play

Is there any other way, we can go about this or is this it?

Will you tell what I told you in the moment of heat?

Will you be honest with me?

When we keep secrets

I never thought we were keeping them between each other, too

Hiding the truth

And now when I see

What was not told to me

I am angry

Because for you I wouldn't have done the same

I wanted a bond where

I can be me

Completely

And you do the same

I wanted to feel safe

Like I could say

And be

Everything that I am

And we would remain true

This didn't mean

You wouldn't explore and I couldn't grow

It just meant that I would know

Without being the butt of the joke

I felt loyal to someone who lied to me

And made me look naïve

As if I was the one who agreed to keep

Everything we do a secret

So that you can seem

Like the man you wish you were

You took advantage

And as private as I am

This could no longer be a secret

I hold

I did something you wouldn't have wanted

I told

Module 8: Sweetheart

In life, you will encounter some sweet, holy, pure and honest people. It is often hard for us to know who to trust and how. Their actions will show you who they are more than their words. Their ability to handle themselves even in discomfort will be a display of who they one-day cold be to you. Be careful of who you push away by not allowing in your space. There are some genuine people who want to see you win but there are also crooks who will smile in your face but wish for your death. The spirit of discernment is pivotal to your growth; prayer is a necessity in order for the truth to be revealed. The more time you spend with God, the easier it will be for you to recognize his voice. It will be difficult because the distraction will try to speak at the same time is God but his voice will be meniscal, sometimes God will upset you with his answer but you must trust his voice.

Sweetheart

Sweetheart I
See so much in you
Sweetheart I
Want so much for you
Sweetheart I
Know it hurts
Sweetheart I
Know it's not what
Sweetheart I
Am here
Sweetheart I
Am not leaving you ever
Sweetheart I
Am your friend
Sweetheart
Mend your broken heart
I will
You are hidden
Protected
And preserved
And I have the nerve to look
For you
To love on you
I want you
And there is nothing you can do
Sweetheart

Just for You

One tasted
One touched
One felt
One love
You would think they've had it
But they can't afford it
Especially with cash
I am special
And so is my a$$
Its mines
I was born with it
But it's not on no cover, girl
I am a rock
Solid, I stand
With water that flows
It gets out of hand
I am but as dry
As my personality sometimes claims
It deserves fame
And if I think for one second
I'll bend
You must've touch these legs that never end
When stretched to capacity
I am like elasticity
I come and I go
You come and you stay
U want to play
With me all day
I am a treat that never gets stale
I hold a gift unlike anything you've seen
I am your dark fantasy and a dream
And everything I've described
God had you in mind
That he made you mine
The gift I carry I'll one-day share with you
I am in possession of something you've wanted to have
And it won't be the last time

You get to access this part of me
I'll give it without questions asked
Cause I now know enough
That what you have is enough for me
I am darn certain God created me
Just for You

Flowers

Pink, purple, yellow, red and green
All in mother nature, scattered throughout
Some big, some little
Some many, some few
With so many abilities
and things to do
your seed is planted
and then you grow
your colors they always show
and people pick you based off things they don't know
you are in a sight unlike any other
many of you around
but for some reason
you stand up
as they sit down
I choose you
Because no matter which one I choose
There is something different about you
You are like a single rose
What you signify is love
You are like sunflower
What you signify is happiness
You are like a lily
What you signify is purity
And those are traits you'll forever carry
So, my flower I love you

Sunshine

Its yellow just like you

Thin and long

Makes me happy

I enjoy it like a song

It is perfection

Not good for me if consumed too much

But perfect if judging off the taste and touch

You're Mine

You look just like me in my younger days

You act like I used to when everybody else would play

You smile like I still smile today

You walk with one leg going in

You are my best friend

You are more than I could've imagined

Smarter than I thought

And funnier, too

Without you

I don't know if life is worth living

You have my eyes

And they only see you

You are my soul

My heart, its true

And I couldn't imagine

Having a better job

Than raising you

I am your mother and proud to say

You're mine and I wouldn't have it any other way

You Should Know

I won't turn my back on you

I won't tell what we've promised or the secrets we hold

I am like your password and I have the code

To unlock everything that you are

I won't call you out of your name

I won't lie

I am to be trusted and I have proved why

With my love, you should know

That you can do anything in the world

You choose

You are my rhythm and blues

And I'm ready to tango with you

Module 9: Comfort

Far too often in life, we become comfortable. We become comfortable with our jobs. Comfortable with our parenting. Comfortable with our knowledge. Comfortable with our giving. Comfortable with our circumstances. Comfortable with lack. Comfortable with not forgiving. Comfortable with how we interact with others. Comfortable with what we say. Comfortable in being everything but who god call us to be. This module of this book pushes you to step outside of what makes you comfortable. We are challenging you to prepare for your next level.

Black Love

I'm thick

He's thicker

You slick

She's slicker

I'm Rich

You Richer

I Love

You Lover

How Come

I can't say No
I promise myself I have to let go
I promise myself I know
But then when asked I do it again
Knowing I said No in my head
Is it my childhood and the sexual abuse that I didn't have an option of saying no to?
Is it the fact that even when I say No
I feel like it happens anyway
So my No has no value
I am weak
I am dumb
I have a reliance on things that has yet to fill this hole and I am unlike anyone I
know
I just keep saying yes
I'm a whole got damn mess
And I know it
I want to say No but I feel like I can't
Like I'm in a restraint
That causes me to choke out the words
Y E S
Even when not at my best and stressed
I will do it
Because I have this thing I have to prove to myself that I'm not all that they said
I'm not crazy
Surprised I'm not dead
I'm not lazy despite what my mother thinks
I am not beautiful but despite what my father said
I am crying as I write this
Because it's deeper than just yes, I will
It is all the things I want and don't have
Hidden behind my I think I'm enough is a girl
Who doesn't quite feel like she deserves to be happy?
At times, feels like she deserves to suffer
And she set her life up to be this way
I keep pushing
Trying to make a way
Feeling like I should take the top off of my Maybach
That I quite don't have

It makes me laugh
Because I'm bold enough to write it
To speak and to say
But my dream I can't keep waiting til the next day
I must say YES to me
And all that I can be
No, all that I am
As I am
I must say YES to every place
That I can go
No, all that I will be
I must say YES to every opportunity
That I come across
I must say YES to my fears
And go afraid
And go afraid
As I may be
I will still go
Cause I can't say No
To all the things I imagined
The hope I felt and needed
I am the YES I've been searching for that will
Fill every hole
With no room
For doubt or fear to slither in
I am filled in a world with sin
And yet I rise
Unlike any phoenix you've ever seen
I am the Dream
That Martin wrote of
I am the YES
That Obama declared
I am the Light
As God created me to be
And yet I asked How Come
How Come it took me to write this to see
That God created me perfectly
So effortlessly
He has done it right
And I can't be surprised

He's God for a reason
This isn't just my season
This is my life line of
Happiness and Love that's going to overflow me
Overtake me
And overfill me
In every capacity possible so how come you haven't?

Protect Your Heart

Behind your back (deep) say bad on your name
It is crazy, you will see
You are being played the fool
{And I sometimes feel sorry for you
And I sometimes feel what I can do
But I am not YOU (deep)}
Smiling and playing
Walking too (sweet)
Your personal business
Shoulda stayed between me and you
See that is something that I would do
Because I don't let everyone into your story
Oh only God the glory that you have
Poor boy, don't you let everyone get next to you
Next to you
Next to you
Next to you
Or in your heart (deep)
Everyone doesn't protect your heart like I will (run)
Like I will
Like I will
Like I have
And I can't get close
Cause there's things I know
That prevents me from being all that I truly am
Don't let no one tell you who to be
Don't let no one control you, even me
Don't let no one tell you when to stop
It's your dream, you gotta go
Reaching for the top

Get Your Self-Esteem Up

Girl, don't you hear him calling you out of ya' name
Girl, don't you see him being the reason you claim
He threats you like you are just a friend
And tells people there's nothing more
But you want so much more
Time to close the door
To your legs
Stop giving these little boys head
Pulling on their dreads
Got the nerve to say
He wanted to have your baby
Just to get you off your goals
Girl, he could care less about you
But you give it to him for free
Feed em' when he's hungry
There when he needs
But will he do the same for you
What does he say when you're not around?
Will he knock your down or tilt your crown?
finish It

I Know My God

I don't know about the way
I don't know about your faith
I don't know about his face
But I know about my God
I don't know about your peace
I just know I will have peace
I don't know about your strength
But I know about my God
I don't know about the way
I don't know about the place
I don't know about the time
But I know about My GOD
I don't know about y'all
But I know about him
About him
About him
My God

Sweet and Low

Oh, Baby
We got that honey, sweet
So sweet as gold
You got the thang that I ain't ever know
And I don't have plans of
Ever letting it go, OH Baby
You are my - Sweet and Low
Sweet and Low is the way we like to go
Do things, our friends ain't Neva seen
We are the - King and Queen
We are the - Dream Team
Called me crazy in my past
Said my relationships would never, ever last but God says I think otherwise
He said KeKe what I have for you is going to be a sweet surprise
And oh my, I can't say that I wish it would've went any other way
The games that I use to play
Crazy things I use to say
We don't ever argue that way
And perfectly, I'd sing this harmony and say
You are the best thing that's ever came my way
Oh, Baby
You ain't perfect
And neither am I
But we got that real love
Nothing artificial about what we do
We love each other and our kids, it's true
We're raising our Princesses, and Princes to be the best that they can be
Have Mommy and a Daddy
I love it when they look at me
Reflection of your love for me
And how low, I'm willing to go for you
I'm willing to show you, boo
So sweet you say it is
I know that's why I got so many kids
Our love to me is irreplaceable
Sweet and Low, Sweet and Low
Oh, Sugar

Bring You Down with Them

Many people get depressed, worried or stressed

The mood around them is naturally gloomy

They pretend to be o.k. but really feels pressured throughout the day

A Love is missing, that 'trying to find

Pretending that it's their the whole time

Wanting to explore something new

Confused and worried about their thoughts

Not caring about one's own happiness

Are you truly happy?

Can you truly find love?

They exude the sadness to all whom their around

Pretending to stand one's ground

Making the situation worse than it is

Trying to have others support on their weird, crazy thoughts

Having battles, having mental and physical faults

Bring you Down with Them

Trying to have you sad, trying to make you mad

No one can smile unless they are

These people truly are insecure

Needing to search within

Needing to find a friend

Someone as an extra caretaker

Someone like a nanny

There for their comforting needs

They keep on fallin'

In and Out of Love

Loving the temporary misery state

Moser Loves Company and Your Just the Company they need

Each Day without Jayde

Lord, How could you do this to me?
You've taken her away from me, without even asking me
He said child, what have I done?
I've taken her away from pain, she's won her battle, Why do you complain?
Cause life just ain't the same
The struggle for her is over but for me, it has just begun and watching my aunt cry,
gives me all the reason to ask you why??
Why have you?
What would you?
Couldn't she live and things still be
Or did I need an angel watching over me?
Our family
It brought us back together
But couldn't she live to storm the weather
Or see whether her work has worked
Her death says it all, she is not an angel who had to fall
She's a Survivor, who survived it all
And God said she's worked so hard in such a short time that she needed a
permanent rest but my tears just won't rest
And the fire inside my chest
Is burning for answers
That cure us here and soon will be released
I promised you that the least
Jayde
You have started something that will never end
And I love and miss you forever
My Best friend

Ambition

I got ambition

Definitely living life on a mission

Never stepping down, but I keep stepping

I got a lot of work on my mind

Working all the time

Showing how I care

Practically living there

My business is my life

I put up with all its strife

Continuing to stay strong

Identifying when I'm wrong

Don't got no time to pout or cry

The road never stops, my mission never dyes

If ever frozen, stuck or confused

I need a laugh to keep me amused

Life goes on with

Ambition

See-Thru

You shined so clear

You were see-thru

You were like a glass window

Accept I only knew

Thru the window, we see the other side; thru you we see the inside

I knew what you said was fake

I know you covered up your mistake

You had everyone tricked and fooled

The only liar and deceiver I knew was you

See-thru it people thought they saw your heart

They thought they found your soul but the true you were cold

Covered with a black tint thru its thickness

It was given a hint

You covered who you were

I saw thru you cause you were see-thru

Get rid of the tint cause it is not truly you

No Trespassing (See-Thru)

I have limits to what you can say

I have limits to what you can do

I have limits to what you can say to me

Don't pass my boundaries

No, Please

I want us succeed

Loving you, loving me

Hitting 1st base, that's just a taste

Tapping 2nd, keeps the pace

Sliding to 3rd, trespassing dirt

Homecoming, keeps it running

It stops on there at that base at that pass- Further going turns to further mistakes

No Trespassing

Rap: Chris Brown went too fast then he had to crawl, Michael went too slow caused his girl to brawl

Were a unit, we are one

We can have so much fun

Just as long as you understand

where you stand

Fully loved

My hair, My Make-up, My Nails, My skin

It's not what makes me, me

Is that all you can see

Treating me like you don't care

I'm here

Not hair

Can't you see true beauty?

Within me, do you know me?

Do you even care?

Tell me my inspiration...

Tell me my aspiration

Tell me my dream

You can't cause

It's all about

My hair, my make-up, My Nails, My skin

Fully Loved

Module 10: Destined

God destined each of us to be somebody who helps somebody in some way, some shape, some form, and some capacity. He blessed us with the talents, gifts, strengths and abilities to change the life of someone. Most of us, including myself have difficulty discovering our destiny. We are often lost on a path that we are unsure where it is taking us but we get up and we go because that is what we are used to. Every conversation you have, every relationship you've formed is ordained by God. We won't know that until we discover the purpose for that relationship, usually way after its ending. God is teaching you something in this very moment while reading this book. He is preparing you for a life only designed for you, Destined by him.

Module 11: PUSH

PUSH acronym for Pray until Something Happens. I never want you to forget these words in your entire life. Not only will you have to PUSH in every aspect of life, sometimes you will have to PUSH when you least expect it, it comes with no warning. Just like the delivery of your baby, you may get a few warning signs to know it's almost time but you may never which PUSH will deliver the baby, through each PUSH, you must never forget to breathe. Breathe with every breath you have in your body. Call on god for every answer, every key and he will provide. Expect good things to come from God.

Forgive Me

Forgive me for not knowing
Forgive me for not sowing
Forgive me for not showing
Forgive me for not hearing
Forgive me for not being
Forgive me son
I love you
I apologize for not being the mother you need
I apologize for not recognizing your needs
You suffered and
I missed the mark
Forgive me for not hugging you
Forgive me for not kissing you
Forgive me for not telling you
Just how great you are
How smart you are
How handsome you are
How enough you are
How mines you are
I love you
Forgive me for I've failed you
Forgive me for I mislead you
Forgive me for I've not always understood
Forgive me for my flaws
Forgive me for you
And I ask the only thing I'd ever want before I leave
Is Can You Please
Forgive Me
I Forgive you for lashing out
I Forgive you for acting out
I Forgive you for the words
I Forgive you for the hurt
As imperfect as I am, I still made you
As imperfect as I am, God still chose me
As imperfect as I am, so are you
And I am your mother

Who will love forever?
There is nothing you can say to make me stop
There is nothing you can do to make me stop
Loving you
Please forgive me

Again

Fuck it up and then leave
I am fucking up
Every opportunity
And then leaving like there wasn't a chance
Like it couldn't be the perfect time to show
Again
I feel fucked up
Cause of someone else's lack
Cause of someone else's shit
And I'm like Am I that Fucked Up
That even I couldn't notice that the situation was fucked up
That the situation was outta order
Not right
Or did I just think about one day
One night
And forget everything else
I'll figure that out later
Man, I should've known
I did know
Can't say I didn't
Or I would be lying
I knew from the very beginning
How my mind felt
How my heart feels
How my body would feel?
And now it is real
Fucked Up
How I expected something different
I think about it pleasantly
Because I stand on my decision proudly
Unlike what I thought I would feel
I left
He left
And I was fucked
But I'm just waiting to get fucked again

Relieve Me

He let me rest

When my head wouldn't

He let me sit

When my heart couldn't

He let me stay

When I wanted to leave

He was my Ibuprofen

That I'd yet to take

Prince of Peace

Stop thinking you look like a reflection of God
When I've seen the faces of your heart
He/she says pray but pleased don't play
Prince of Peace
{Chorus: Oh, Prince of Peace come over me
Fill me with the joy of God
Prophetess spoke from her heart
The word of God
The word- Word of God
Lift my hands to you~~ Jesus, reaching for your glory and praise
Something that I need every day}
Stop thinking that the doctor has the last day
Break_ Chains - We command you
Like Tasha would said "Death lies on the power of your tongue"
So break that chain, I command you to break
Stop believing everything that you hear, it's God telling you that he's here
His word is final
Prince of Peace, that's what they call me (God says)
I am the Almighty
All the night I have comes from my hands
Power, they think I have- Only for a small amount of time will it lasts if they don't
give honor to me
I am the Almighty (God says)
Oh, when he speaks your ears to say but it could change the way
Prince of Peace
Lord, cover me
Through the disgruntled pouts of a bipolar man
Like a beach does water to the sand
Like a homeless man does the trash can
I reach but only so high without your power
I lose my wings to fly
That's why, I bow at your presence
Your so excellent
Strong hold you'll be forever
They ain't Eva gotta ask one question out of me
Who is that you'd love to be?
The Prince of Peace

She's Here

I carry her for months

Clothes picked out and ready to wear

Pampers stacked

Family all waiting to see her pretty face

Daddy hopes she looks just like me

But I've gotta feeling she'll be his twin

They show me her heartbeat

And her feet in a sonogram

I post it on the gram

Just waiting for her arrival

My water breaks

I contract

And the centimeters are growing

She's here

But the worry on the doctor's face frightens me

Something is not right

I don't hear her cries

And she's being taken away

Then silence

Silent cries

As the doctor and a team of nurses says I'm sorry

We tried to revive her but she no longer has a heartbeat

My heart beats

Almost out of my chest

Wondering how

Module 12: Next Level

The next level will come with new devils. It will bring the ultimate strength out of you. Growth is going to take a strong level of faith, dedication, honor and love to get. It will require a new mindset, a new focus and a lot of sacrifices. Many of the sacrifices, you will wish you can avoid but they will be very present. Storm after storm will come but sun after sun will shine. Don't allow your circumstances to control you, you control your circumstances. You are the key to your next level. Who are you willing to remove from your life? Who are you willing to stop speaking to? What are you willing to give UP?

<u>*Exposed*</u>

I'm crying yet again
Feeling left again
No family. No man.
No money. No job.
I work so hard
Or at least I feel I do
It may not seem like work to you
But I move my feet in ways
That you couldn't compare
My hands I bare
At work, they're there
And I am twenty-two
Feeling like what should I do?
I have ousted every resource in my life
And there is still so much needed in my life
New tires. New battery. Alignment and more
This is a story that few only know.
I've been struggling so long, it doesn't show
To others but my accounts see it, my hands do too and my restless nights, without
an allergy pill what would I do?
I am begging the lord for all that I've been promised
But yet
My life feels like it's no longer moving.
At times, it was going and going so fast, I was doing and doing so fast but now the
dreaded moments last
And yet I still am almost twenty-three
This can't be me
The girl who promised herself to be
A billionaire
Before Twenty-three
Can barely pay her car note and insurance
Without having little left
I am stressed
And I can't deny
I keep asking God why
Do I do so much but yet I am still lacking?
God says Breathe and I do then tears fall again
He's releasing me

From me
I have a hold on the gift God has yet to unfold and I don't know why
But I'm going to breathe my way through this overwhelming feeling
I can't let it hold me down forever
My fear of exposing all that I am
My fear of loving him
My fear that I won't succeed
Or be okay
God is saying
I gotchu Marshay
Do it anyway
My fear of saying "yes"
My fear of facing "no"
My fear of actually letting go
To what isn't and accepting what is
He said it
I knew it
It was true
She said it
I told him
I felt it
It was true
The release of unknown secrets is something I do
I tell on me before you can
I open my mouth and I express my thoughts, my feelings with no regrets
I am not purposely entertaining when I state how I feel
I am real
Is not a statement I have to make?
Because my soul and its purpose you couldn't take
And you damn sure couldn't fake
It is who I am
A living testimony
Thanks to him
My God, I have never seen fail me
My God, I have failed
And promise to prevail
In every dark day and bright one too
I am a representation of him and it's beautiful
One you have never seen before
I sit sad because at 22, I don't have my own room

My own space but let others tell it, my life is so great
I think it's laced to show a face that only you can see
But what's really behind only few will know
The struggle they speak of
I could relate
My fate
I see it
I feel it
I know it's coming but just not now
And I am around
Going, moving and being
I've been down but still held you up
I've been low but your still pushed you forward
I've been crying but I still helped you out
I am all the things I thought I could not
But what I see in my future
Is the reaps of every seed I've sown
Every plant I've grown
Every vision I own
And just like every lie you tell
I am being exposed
For the heart I have
For the times I've cried
For the prayers I've prayed
For the time I struggled
For the times I lacked
God has had my back
Even when I barely was holding up my own
I am being exposed
For the little girl who wanted and didn't have
For the grown woman who desires but doesn't have
I am being exposed
For the dreamer
The warrior
The lover
The way maker
The giant
The small
The lovely
The all

I am being exposed
As this creation that only God could form
So rare in all its purity
I form
A soul unlike any this earth seems to bare
I am here
And I don't plan on leaving anytime soon
I am warmth
Even though my hands are cold
I am strength
Even when tears bare my face
I am grace
Even when I've repeated mistakes
And I am here
Through every breath I breathe
I see just why
God decided to allow me to live
And I am his
Thank you
My God for making me unafraid to show my real
Now my heart, Can you feel?
Exposed

Make Me Over Again

I am overwhelmed with emotion
I just want to cry
And I don't have one specific reason why
But I
Am just tired of wanting more than I have
I am tired of pushing
And as rude is it may be, I am tired of praying
I am tired of thinking of what they said God had for me, would one day be mines
I am tired of being a girl with ambition and possibilities
But the opportunity just never seems to come
I am done with saying if I had just
I am done with thinking well maybe I need to
There is nothing else that I can say or do
I feel I have done all I can
I have said what was necessary for me to say
And I am doing my best
At trying to hold it together
Even though, I feel like I want to lay on someone's lap and cry
I want Iyanla to hold me
And say "yeah, baby, let it out"
I know, I don't want anyone to feel sorry for me
As if I do not have two feet
Two hands
Two ears
Two eyes
And a mouth
I am not a victim of my circumstances
I will not pretend like my situation did something to me
I will not think that someone around me owes me something
I owe it all to myself
To work harder
I am pissed
It's one thing then another and then another
I used to work so hard in school
Finish my homework while in class
Go home, be quiet, and speak last
And I would not have friends

Not talk
Barely walk
The halls
Only to class
Carry book bags filled with heavy books
And turn my head
Every time a boy looked
But where am I now
Stuck without a college degree
No high paying earnings
Or income to rely on
I pushed myself to be my best while in school
Missing so many days cause I hate following rules
But I know that when there, I don't do anything else but what I was told
I wrote
I counted
I learned
I earned
Every grade
And every award
But this is my reward
A life I don't think anyone deserves
I don't have no kids
No husband
No man
As I once imagined I would
I don't have no job
No check
No income
That I can guarantee
No I am not the best version of me
At this time
There are things I feel I still need to do
A couple of things I've always wanted to come true
But how
I keep going to God
Begging please
On my knees
God Help Me!

<u>Origin</u>

We are all some superstars
In our unique way
God created Marshay
There's a reason your small and a reason your tall
At one point, we all have to crawl
We learn to walk and run
Usually by the age of one
Cause 4 us, Life has just begun
We are all some superstars
Each created Bizarre
With our own Memoir
We originated from the best and our Kings and Queens none the less

Bold Enough

Who would've dare thought you were
BOLD ENOUGH
To have her answer the phone and say
BOLD ENOUGH
To claim she'd been at my home today
BOLD ENOUGH
To say you don't need me and don't want to be with me
BOLD ENOUGH
To say you're coming to get your stuff
BOLD ENOUGH
To believe anything here is yours
BOLD ENOUGH
TO need me and ask for my help four months later
WELL, IVE HAD ENOUGH (background: BOLD ENOUGH) whisper

Future

One day you're born
One day you die
One day you live
One day you cry
One day you see
One day you try
One day you lie
One day you give
One day you sow
One day you'll know

<u>Grace</u>

Only few are granted this by our most gracious God
Everyone is forgiven
But not everyone is offered grace
Grace covers you during your wrong
Protects you during your sin
Grace is that friend that always lies for you
Just when you need
Without you asking
Grace doesn't just lend a hand
But takes the fault for your wrongdoing
You want it
But not everyone has it
In the time, where it could've turned out differently
You thank him because it turned out like it should
And you thank him for being the God of I Could

Next Level

My hair no longer in stage 2

My heart is ready for more

My life is going well

But I'm ready for more

I want my edges back

I want my credit back, too

I want you back

And us back

And I know it sounds like I'm trying to go back

But without fixing the odds that were meant to win

I am just human

And filled with sin

Unmatched on this earth today

I can say

There are a few pieces that I have to take with me when I move

And that includes you

www.ingramcontent.com/pod-product-compliance
Lightning Source LLC
Chambersburg PA
CBHW081632040426

42449CB00014B/3269